I0505280

Mastering Day Trading:
A Beginners Guide to Profitable Trading

R.C. Investments

Table of Contents

Introduction to Day Trading

In recent years, day trading has become an increasingly popular form of investment. It involves buying and selling financial instruments within a single trading day, with the goal of profiting from small price fluctuations. Unlike long-term investors, day traders are not interested in holding onto their investments for weeks or months. Instead, they seek to capitalize on short-term price movements to generate quick profits.

The Basics of Day Trading:

Day trading involves buying and selling financial instruments, such as stocks, options, futures, or currencies, within a single trading day. A day trader typically seeks to profit from small price movements in these instruments. They might buy a stock when its price is low and sell it a few hours later when its price has risen, for example.

Day traders often use technical analysis to identify trends in the market and determine when to enter and exit trades. Technical analysis involves using charts and indicators to analyze past price movements and predict future ones. Day traders may also use fundamental analysis to evaluate the financial health and prospects of a particular company or industry.

Why Day Trading Can Be Profitable:

Day trading can be an attractive form of investment because it offers the potential for high returns. By buying and selling financial instruments quickly, day traders can generate profits in a short amount of time. This is especially true in volatile markets, where prices can fluctuate rapidly and unpredictably.

Another advantage of day trading is the ability to use leverage. Many day traders use margin accounts, which allow them to borrow money from their broker to increase their buying power. This can magnify potential profits, but it also increases the risk of losses.

In addition, day trading can be a flexible and convenient way to make money. Unlike long-term investors, day traders do not need to commit large amounts of time to their investments. They can trade from anywhere with an internet connection, and they can choose how many trades they want to make in a day.

The Risks of Day Trading:

While day trading can be profitable, it is also a high-risk form of investment. Because day traders seek to profit from small price movements, they must make frequent trades to generate significant profits. This can increase the risk of losses, as each trade carries its own set of costs and risks.

Another risk of day trading is the potential for emotional decision-making. Because day traders make quick decisions based on rapidly changing market conditions, they can be susceptible to fear and greed. This can lead them to make impulsive trades that result in losses.

In addition, day traders must contend with a number of other risks, including market volatility, technical glitches, and regulatory changes. The market can be unpredictable, and unexpected events can cause prices to fluctuate rapidly. Technical glitches can cause trades to be executed incorrectly, and regulatory changes can limit the types of investments that day traders can make.

How This Book Can Help:

This book is designed to help beginner day traders understand the basics of day trading, develop a solid trading plan, and manage the risks associated with this form of investment. It will cover everything from setting up a trading account to executing trades and managing emotions.

In the following chapters, readers will learn how to choose a broker, understand trading terminology, and analyze market trends. They will also learn how to develop a trading plan that aligns with their goals and objectives, and they will discover strategies for minimizing risk and maximizing profits.

Throughout the book, readers will be provided with practical advice, real-world examples, and clear explanations of key concepts. They will learn how to execute trades using different types of orders, read charts, and identify entry and exit points.

In addition, this book will cover advanced trading strategies, such as scalping, swing trading, and position trading. Readers will also learn how to manage emotions and stay disciplined, avoiding the fear and Chapter 1: Introduction to Day Trading

In recent years, day trading has become an increasingly popular form of investment. It involves buying and selling financial instruments within a single trading day, with the goal of profiting from small price fluctuations. Unlike long-term investors, day traders are not interested in holding onto their investments for weeks or months. Instead, they seek to capitalize on short-term price movements to generate quick profits.

Chapter 1: Getting Started

If you're new to day trading, the first step is to set up a trading account with a broker. A trading account is a special type of account that allows you to buy and sell financial instruments, such as stocks, options, futures, or currencies.

Setting Up a Trading Account:

Setting up a trading account is a relatively straightforward process. Most brokers offer online account applications that can be completed in a matter of minutes. To open an account, you will typically need to provide some basic personal information, such as your name, address, and social security number. You may also need to provide information about your employment and income.

Once your account is set up, you will need to fund it before you can start trading. Most brokers offer a variety of funding options, such as bank transfers, credit cards, or electronic payment methods.

Choosing a Broker:

Choosing the right broker is crucial to your success as a day trader. A broker is a company or individual that acts as an intermediary between you and the financial markets. They provide you with access to trading platforms, research tools, and other resources that can help you make informed trading decisions.

When choosing a broker, it's important to consider a variety of factors, such as their fees, trading platforms, customer support, and regulatory status. Some brokers specialize in certain types of financial instruments, so it's important to choose a broker that offers the types of instruments you want to trade.

(Some online brokers include Robinhood, Webull, Moomoo, etc.)

Understanding Trading Terminology:

As a day trader, it's important to understand the terminology used in the financial markets. Some common trading terms include:

Bid:
The highest price a buyer is willing to pay for a financial instrument.

Ask:
The lowest price a seller is willing to accept for a financial instrument.

Spread:
The difference between the bid and ask prices.

Volume:
The number of shares or contracts traded in a given period of time.

Liquidity:
The ease with which a financial instrument can be bought or sold without affecting its price.

Order:
A request to buy or sell a financial instrument at a certain price.

Understanding Stock Market Hours:

The stock market is only open for trading during certain hours of the day. In the United States, the stock market is open from 9:30 a.m. to 4:00 p.m. Eastern Time, Monday through Friday. However, some brokers may offer extended trading hours, allowing you to trade before or after the official market hours.

It's important to understand the stock market hours in your time zone so you can plan your trading accordingly. Keep in mind that different financial instruments may have different trading hours, so be sure to check with your broker for specific trading hours.

In the next chapter, we'll explore how to analyze the financial markets and identify potential trading opportunities. By understanding the basics of technical and fundamental analysis, you can make informed trading decisions and increase your chances of success as a day trader.

Chapter 2: Understanding Market Analysis

As a day trader, your success depends on your ability to analyze the financial markets and identify potential trading opportunities. There are two main approaches to market analysis: technical analysis and fundamental analysis.

Technical Analysis:

Technical analysis is the study of past market data, such as price and volume, to identify patterns and trends that can help predict future price movements. Technical analysts use charts and other tools to analyze market data and identify potential trading opportunities.

Some common technical analysis tools include:

Moving averages:
A moving average is a line that represents the average price of a financial instrument over a certain period of time. Moving averages can help identify trends and support and resistance levels.

Chart patterns:
Chart patterns are formations that appear on a price chart and can indicate potential price movements. Some

common chart patterns include triangles, head and shoulders, and double tops and bottoms.

Oscillators:
Oscillators are indicators that measure the momentum of price movements. Some common oscillators include the Relative Strength Index (RSI) and the Moving Average Convergence Divergence (MACD) indicator.

Fundamental Analysis:

Fundamental analysis is the study of economic and financial factors, such as earnings reports, interest rates, and industry trends, that can affect the value of a financial instrument. Fundamental analysts use this information to assess the intrinsic value of a financial instrument and make trading decisions based on that assessment.

Some common fundamental analysis tools include:

Financial statements:
Financial statements, such as income statements and balance sheets, provide information about a company's financial performance and can be used to assess its value.

Economic indicators:
Economic indicators, such as Gross Domestic Product (GDP) and inflation rates, provide information about the overall health of the economy and can be used to assess the value of financial instruments.

Industry trends:
Industry trends, such as changes in consumer behavior or new technological developments, can affect the value of financial instruments in that industry.

Using News and Market Trends:

In addition to technical and fundamental analysis, day traders can also use news and market trends to identify potential trading opportunities. News events, such as earnings reports or political developments, can affect the value of financial instruments and create opportunities for trading.

Market trends, such as changes in consumer behavior or technological developments, can also create opportunities for trading. By staying informed about news and market trends, day traders can identify potential trading opportunities and make informed trading decisions.

In the next chapter, we'll explore how to develop a trading plan and manage risk. By developing a solid trading plan and using risk management strategies, you can minimize your losses and maximize your profits as a day trader.

Chapter 3: Developing a Trading Plan

Once you have a basic understanding of market analysis, it's time to start developing your trading plan. A trading plan is a set of rules and guidelines that you will follow when making trades. A well-developed trading plan can help you achieve your trading goals and minimize your risk.

Setting Goals and Objectives:

The first step in developing a trading plan is to set your goals and objectives. This will help you determine what you want to achieve as a trader and how you will measure your success. Your goals and objectives should be specific, measurable, and realistic.

For example, you might set a goal to make a certain amount of profit each month or to achieve a certain win-loss ratio. Whatever your goals and objectives, make sure they are realistic and achievable.

Defining Trading Strategies:

The next step in developing a trading plan is to define your trading strategies. Your trading strategies should be based on your analysis of the financial markets and your goals and objectives as a trader. There are many different trading strategies, and the best strategy for you will depend on your personal preferences and trading style.

Some common trading strategies include:

Scalping: Scalping is a trading strategy that involves making many small trades over a short period of time, typically a few seconds to a few minutes.

Day trading: Day trading is a trading strategy that involves buying and selling financial instruments within the same trading day.

Swing trading: Swing trading is a trading strategy that involves holding positions for a few days to a few weeks, in order to take advantage of market trends.

Risk Management:

Finally, it's important to incorporate risk management into your trading plan. Risk management is the process of identifying and minimizing the risks associated with trading.

Some common risk management strategies include:

Setting stop-loss orders:
A stop-loss order is an order that automatically closes a trade if the price of the financial instrument reaches a certain level. Stop-loss orders can help limit your losses if the market moves against you.

Using position sizing:
Position sizing is the process of determining how much to invest in each trade. By using position sizing, you can limit your risk exposure and minimize your losses.

Diversifying your portfolio:
Diversification is the process of investing in a variety of financial instruments, in order to spread your risk across different markets and industries.

By developing a solid trading plan and using risk management strategies, you can minimize your losses and maximize your profits as a day trader. In the next chapter, we'll explore how to execute trades and manage your trading platform.

Chapter 4: Executing Trades

Now that you have developed your trading plan and have a good understanding of market analysis, it's time to start executing trades. In this chapter, we'll explore the different types of orders you can place, how to read charts, and how to identify entry and exit points.

Types of Orders:

When placing a trade, there are several types of orders you can use. The type of order you choose will depend on your trading strategy and your goals and objectives as a trader. Here are some common types of orders:

Market order:
A market order is an order to buy or sell a financial instrument at the current market price. Market orders are executed immediately.

Limit order:
A limit order is an order to buy or sell a financial instrument at a specified price. If the market price does not reach the specified price, the trade will not be executed.

Stop order:
A stop order is an order to buy or sell a financial instrument once the market price reaches a specified price. Stop orders are often used as a risk management tool to limit losses.

Reading Charts:

Charts are an essential tool for day traders. They provide a visual representation of market trends and price movements. There are several types of charts, but the most common type is the candlestick chart. A candlestick chart shows the opening and closing prices, as well as the high and low prices, for a particular period of time.

When reading charts, it's important to look for patterns and trends. Some common patterns include:

Support and resistance levels:
Support and resistance levels are price levels where the market has historically had difficulty moving past. They can be used to identify potential entry and exit points.

Trend lines:
Trend lines are lines drawn on a chart to connect two or more price points. They can be used to identify market trends and potential entry and exit points.

Moving averages:
Moving averages are lines drawn on a chart to represent the average price of a financial instrument over a specified period of time. They can be used to identify market trends and potential entry and exit points.

Identifying Entry and Exit Points:

Once you have a good understanding of market analysis and have read charts, it's time to start identifying entry and exit points for your trades. Entry and exit points are the prices at which you will buy and sell financial instruments.

There are several strategies for identifying entry and exit points, but here are a few common ones:

Breakout strategy:

A breakout strategy involves buying a financial instrument when it breaks through a support or resistance level, and selling it when it reaches the next level.

Moving average strategy:
A moving average strategy involves buying a financial instrument when its price crosses above its moving average, and selling it when its price crosses below its moving average.

Trend following strategy:
A trend following strategy involves buying a financial instrument when it's in an uptrend, and selling it when it's in a downtrend.

By using a combination of different strategies and techniques, you can identify entry and exit points that work best for your trading style and goals. In the next chapter, we'll explore how to manage your trades and analyze your performance as a day trader.

Chapter 5: Advanced Trading Strategies

Now that you have a solid understanding of the basics of day trading, it's time to explore some advanced trading strategies. In this chapter, we'll discuss three common advanced trading strategies: scalping, swing trading, and position trading.

Scalping:

Scalping is a high-frequency trading strategy that involves making numerous trades throughout the day with the goal of making small profits on each trade. Scalpers look for opportunities to buy and sell financial instruments within seconds or minutes of each other, taking advantage of small price movements.

To be successful at scalping, traders need to have a good understanding of market trends and be able to identify entry and exit points quickly. Scalping requires a high level of discipline and focus, as traders need to be able to make split-second decisions.

Swing Trading:

Swing trading is a trading strategy that involves holding financial instruments for several days or even weeks, with the goal of taking advantage of medium-term price movements. Swing traders look for opportunities to buy and sell financial instruments based on market trends and price patterns.

To be successful at swing trading, traders need to be able to identify market trends and have a good understanding of technical analysis. Swing trading requires a level of patience and discipline, as traders need to be able to hold onto positions for several days or weeks.

Position Trading:

Position trading is a long-term trading strategy that involves holding financial instruments for several months or even years, with the goal of taking advantage of long-term price movements. Position traders look for opportunities to buy and hold financial instruments based on market trends and fundamental analysis.

To be successful at position trading, traders need to have a good understanding of market trends and economic indicators. Position trading requires a high level of patience and discipline, as traders need to be able to hold onto positions for several months or years.

Choosing the Right Strategy:

Choosing the right trading strategy is crucial to your success as a day trader. The strategy you choose will depend on your trading style, goals, and risk tolerance. Some traders prefer the fast-paced action of scalping, while others prefer the longer-term approach of position trading.

It's important to experiment with different strategies and find the one that works best for you. Remember, there's no one-size-fits-all approach to trading. What works for one trader may not work for another. In the next chapter, we'll explore how to manage risk and protect your trading capital.

Chapter 6: Managing Emotions

As a day trader, managing your emotions is just as important as managing your trades. Emotions such as fear, greed, and excitement can cloud your judgment and lead to impulsive decisions that can result in losses. In this chapter, we'll discuss how to stay disciplined, control your emotions, and avoid impulsive decisions.

Staying Disciplined:

Staying disciplined is crucial to your success as a day trader. This means sticking to your trading plan, following your trading strategies, and avoiding impulsive decisions. It's important to have a set of rules and guidelines that you follow consistently. This will help you stay focused and make rational decisions.

Controlling Fear and Greed:

Fear and greed are two of the most common emotions that traders experience. Fear can lead to hesitation and missed opportunities, while greed can lead to impulsive decisions and taking unnecessary risks. It's important to keep these emotions in check and make decisions based on logic and analysis, rather than emotion.

One way to control fear and greed is to set realistic goals and objectives. This will help you stay focused and avoid getting carried away by short-term gains or losses. It's also important to remember that losses are a natural part of trading and to not let them affect your emotions or cloud your judgment.

Avoiding Impulsive Decisions:

Impulsive decisions can be the downfall of many day traders. It's important to take the time to analyze the market and make informed decisions, rather than acting on impulse. This means avoiding chasing trends or making decisions based on rumors or hearsay.

One way to avoid impulsive decisions is to have a trading plan that includes entry and exit points. This will help you stay focused and avoid making decisions based on emotion or impulse.

Managing your emotions is a crucial part of being a successful day trader. Staying disciplined, controlling your emotions, and avoiding impulsive decisions will help you make rational decisions and increase your chances of success. By following the guidelines outlined in this chapter, you can become a more disciplined and focused day trader. In the next chapter, we'll discuss how to keep your trading capital safe and manage risk.

Chapter 7: Resources and Tools

As a day trader, having the right tools and resources can make all the difference in your success. In this chapter, we'll discuss the essential tools and resources that every day trader should have access to.

Trading Platforms:

A trading platform is software that allows you to execute trades and monitor market activity. There are many trading platforms available, each with its own features and benefits. It's important to choose a platform that suits your needs and trading style.

Some popular trading platforms include Thinkorswim, Interactive Brokers, and MetaTrader 4. Each platform has its own strengths and weaknesses, so it's important to do your research and choose one that works for you.

Charting Software:

Charting software is essential for day traders, as it allows you to analyze market trends and identify potential trades. There are many charting software options available, both free and paid. Some popular charting software includes TradingView, MetaTrader 4, and TC2000.

Trading Communities and Resources:

Trading communities and resources can be invaluable for day traders. They offer a wealth of information, support, and guidance. Joining a trading community can provide you with access to experienced traders who can offer advice and share their strategies.

There are many trading communities available, both online and offline. Some popular online communities include Reddit's r/Daytrading and Elite Trader. There are also many trading resources available, such as books, webinars, and courses. It's important to do your research and choose resources that are reputable and suited to your needs.

Having the right tools and resources is crucial to your success as a day trader. Trading platforms, charting software, and trading communities and resources can all provide you with valuable insights and support. By using the tools and resources outlined in this chapter, you can increase your chances of success and become a more effective day trader. In the next chapter, we'll discuss how to evaluate your performance and make adjustments to your trading plan.

Conclusion:

In this book, we've covered the basics of day trading, the risks and rewards, and how to develop a successful trading plan. We've discussed market analysis, trading strategies, risk management, and the importance of managing your emotions. We've also explored the tools and resources that every day trader needs to have at their disposal.

Now that you've learned the key concepts of day trading, it's time to take the next steps towards success. It's important to remember that day trading requires dedication, discipline, and continuous learning. By implementing the strategies and techniques outlined in this book and continuously honing your skills, you can achieve success in the world of day trading.

Remember that day trading can be a challenging and sometimes unpredictable venture. It's important to stay focused on your goals and remain disciplined in your approach. Keep in mind that losses are inevitable, but they can be minimized through effective risk management and a well-developed trading plan.

In the end I hope that this book has provided you with a solid foundation for your day trading journey. Always remember to stay informed, be disciplined, and never stop learning. With dedication and hard work, you can become a successful day trader. Good luck!

www.ingramcontent.com/pod-product-compliance
Lightning Source LLC
Chambersburg PA
CBHW072240230526
45466CB00025B/2214